BEST OF
FISH
A Taste of the Seven Seas

GARDEN *of* **GRAPES.**

Introduction

Ladies and gentlemen, wanderers of the culinary cosmos, and fellow seekers of that elusive perfect bite, I raise my glass – not of some fancy wine, mind you, but of good old human connection – to welcome you to a journey through the briny depths and aquatic wonders that grace our planet's platter.

As you hold this book in your hands, let me assure you, it's not just a cookbook. It's a ticket to voyage without the jet lag, an expedition that spans continents and cultures, all from the comfort of your humble abode. We're about to dive headfirst into a sea of flavors, a piscine panorama that showcases the best fish dishes humanity has to offer – a collection that's been simmering in my thoughts and travels for quite some time now.

In those dimly lit taverns of Tokyo, where the scent of freshly caught Tsukiji fish mingles with the laughter of chefs, or along the bustling markets of Marrakech, where the sea's bounty marries the richness of North African spices – in these places and countless others, I've found my inspiration. It's the untiring fishermen who brave the tempestuous waves and the skilled cooks who turn their catch into poetry on a plate – they're the true heroes here. And I'm just the storyteller, the one fortunate enough to bring their tales to your kitchen.

Expect no ordinary cookbook, my friends. Oh no, we're not just talking recipes here. We're embarking on a sensory expedition, a narrative woven with anecdotes, cultural tidbits, and a genuine quest for that elusive umami symphony. Picture this: recipes that have journeyed through generations, infused with the essence of time and tradition, yet tweaked for the modern seeker of flavor. And fear not, for whether you're a seasoned chef or someone whose idea of cooking is boiling water for pasta, there's a place for you at this table.

So, consider this your invitation to a globetrotting, net-casting, line-dancing exploration of taste. Open these pages with an open heart, a hungry stomach, and a willingness to embrace the unknown – because, dear reader, we're about to embark on a fishy adventure that'll make you see the world, and its flavors, in a way you've never imagined.

Steamed Fish with Ginger and Soy
See page, 91

Cooking Philosophy or Approach

Now, before we wade into the culinary shallows, let me share a glimpse of my approach to food, cooking, and the art of savoring life's little pleasures. You see, my philosophy is one of unapologetic authenticity – a celebration of imperfections, a bow to the unfiltered moments that flavor our experiences.

In these recipes, you won't find a rigid set of rules etched in stone tablets. No, my friends, what you'll find are flexible roadmaps, mere suggestions to guide you on your flavor expedition. Because, let's face it, some days you might want a dash of daring experimentation, while others might call for the comforting embrace of the familiar.

I've always believed that the true essence of cooking lies not just in the final dish, but in the journey itself. It's in the sizzle of a hot pan that whispers promises of crispiness, the aroma that escapes a pot of simmering broth and fills your kitchen with stories of faraway lands. It's in those moments when you dare to deviate from the recipe, adding a pinch of your personality to the mix.

Now, as for the techniques, ingredients, and styles that will dance across these pages – brace yourselves, because it's going to be a whirlwind tour. From the delicate art of ceviche that lets citrus kiss fish to perfection, to the fiery embrace of a Thai chili paste that'll set your taste buds on a rollercoaster ride. You'll find yourself sautéing, grilling, and perhaps even raw-curing your way through this adventure.

But let me tell you, it's not just about what happens in the pan or on the grill. It's about the stories behind each technique, the tales spun by generations who've perfected these methods through trial, error, and maybe a happy accident or two. It's about understanding why a certain spice blend is the heartbeat of a coastal village, or why a specific cooking vessel has been cherished for centuries.

So, my fellow flavor aficionados, get ready to roll up your sleeves, dust off those cutting boards, and embark on a gastronomic escapade that'll tease your senses and broaden your culinary horizons. Because in this cookbook, it's not just about the recipes – it's about the voyage, the laughter shared over a chopping board, the joy of discovering the alchemy that happens when flavors collide.

Let's dive in, shall we? The sea of flavors awaits, and I promise you, it's going to be an expedition worth savoring.

General Cooking Tips and Techniques

Alright, my culinary comrades, gather 'round for some nifty nuggets of kitchen wisdom that are going to make your fishy endeavors smoother than a well-oiled skillet.

1. Choose Wisely, Cook Confidently: When it comes to selecting your fish, let your senses be your guide. Look for clear, vibrant eyes, glistening skin, and a briny scent of the ocean. Trust me, your nose knows best.

2. The Art of Prepping: Before you dive into the cooking frenzy, give your fish a little spa treatment. Scale it, gut it, and trim any ragged edges. Pat it dry with the care of a gentle breeze, ensuring a crisp sear that'll make your taste buds dance.

3. Heat Mastery: When pan-searing, grilling, or even roasting, make friends with high heat. We're talking sizzling symphonies and mouthwatering caramelization. Just remember, high heat, a touch of oil, and a bit of patience – don't flip your fish too soon or you'll break their sear-loving hearts.

4. The Marinade Tango: If you're thinking marinades, be kind to your seafood. Acidic marinades, like citrus juices, love to tenderize fish. But too much time in the bath, and you'll end up with ceviche on your hands. Aim for balance, a delicate dance between flavor infusion and texture preservation.

5. Spice Odyssey: Spices are your passport to global flavor. Dive into the world of spice rubs, pastes, and blends. Just remember, a pinch can transport your dish, while a handful can hijack the show. So, go easy, taste as you go, and let your taste buds navigate the route

6. Friends of Simplicity: While we're all for culinary exploration, sometimes the simple path is the most enchanting. A sprinkle of sea salt, a twist of pepper, a drizzle of quality olive oil – these are the companions that let the fish shine in all its glory.

7. Doneness Dilemma: The age-old question: When is fish done? Here's a tip – trust your instincts. Fish turns opaque and flakes easily when cooked through. And if you're unsure, just sneak a peek with a fork. It's not a heist; it's quality control.

8. The Rest is Magic: Once your fish has graced the heat, let it take a breather before you pounce. Resting allows the juices to redistribute, giving you moist, succulent bites that'll make your taste buds throw a party.

Ingredient Selection, Preparation, and Cooking Methods

When it comes to ingredients, my friends, the ocean is your oyster – pun intended. Seek the freshest catch you can lay your hands on, and if you're landlocked, don't hesitate to go frozen. Frozen fish can often lock in that just-caught essence.

Prepare with purpose. Be it a quick ceviche or a slow-cooked stew, embrace the process. Take the time to marinate, chop, and arrange your ingredients with love – because trust me, that love finds its way into every mouthful.

As for cooking methods, flip through these pages with an open mind. Pan-fry for the crispy, grill for the smoky, bake for the gentle touch. Each method brings its own character to the plate, so let your mood and the occasion guide your choice.

Remember, my fellow flavor explorers, this cookbook is your treasure map, your secret guide to unlocking the treasures of the sea. So go forth with confidence, wield your spatula like a sword, and let your taste buds be your North Star. The ocean's bounty is waiting to be discovered in your very own kitchen – so set sail, and may your culinary adventures be as bold as your appetite.

Kitchen Essentials:

Ah, my comrades-in-cooking, before we embark on our flavor odyssey, let's take a moment to ensure you're armed with the right tools – your trusty shipmates as you navigate the culinary seas.

1. Chef's Knife: Consider this your first mate. A sharp, sturdy chef's knife is your ticket to slicing, dicing, and conquering ingredients with finesse. Keep it honed and your fingers well clear.

2. Cutting Board: A reliable, spacious cutting board is your canvas. Wood or plastic, it's where your ingredients transform from mere edibles to works of culinary art.

3. Non-Stick Skillet: For those quick sears and sautés, a non-stick skillet is your wingman. Ensure it's hot and ready before introducing your fish – that sizzle is music to our ears.

4. Grill Pan: If you're yearning for those grill marks, a grill pan is your answer. Preheat it to those sizzling temps, and remember, patience is the secret behind those picturesque lines.

5. Ovenproof Baking Dish: From bakes to roasts, a good ovenproof dish is your partner-in-crime. Make sure it's well-seasoned to prevent sticking and deliver effortless release.

6. Citrus Juicer: When life gives you lemons (or limes or oranges), a citrus juicer is your squeeze machine. Extract that liquid gold for marinades, dressings, or a zesty finish.

7. Tongs: Channel your inner Neptune with a pair of sturdy tongs. They're your graspers of fish fillets, turning them with grace and precision.

8. Fish Spatula: This one's like a gentle sea breeze – a fish spatula. Its thin, flexible edge glides under delicate fillets, ensuring they stay intact and pristine.

9. Thermometer: If you're dancing with large fish cuts or simply crave precision, a kitchen thermometer is your compass. It leads you to the promised land of perfect doneness.

10. Mixing Bowls: These are your vessels of creation. From marinating to tossing salads, mixing bowls are your partners in combining flavors with love.

11. Measuring Cups and Spoons: When recipes call for a dash of accuracy, these are your trusty navigational tools. Follow the measurements, and your culinary voyage will be smooth sailing.

12. Microplane Zester: For those aromatic zest shavings, a microplane zester is your secret weapon. It extracts the essence without delving into the bitterness.

13. Fish Scaler: If your fish comes with scales, this tool is your armor. It's like giving your fish a makeover, revealing that shiny, pristine skin underneath.

14. Fish Platter: Present your masterpieces with flair on a fish platter. It's like giving your creations a stage, where they can bask in admiration before meeting their delicious fate.

Tips on How to Use These Tools Effectively

Keep your knives sharp. A dull blade is a recipe for accidents.

Preheat your pans and skillets before introducing your fish. That initial sizzle is a sign of culinary success.

Use tongs and spatulas gently, especially when handling delicate fish. You're not wrestling; you're coaxing.

Measure ingredients accurately – precision is key, especially in recipes that dance on the edge of flavor balance.

Make use of mixing bowls to prep and organize your ingredients before you dive into cooking. This makes the process smoother and more enjoyable.

Treat your ovenproof baking dishes with care. A well-seasoned dish ensures easy food release.

When zesting citrus, go for the outermost layer of the peel. The pith beneath can be bitter and overpowering.

Don't fear the fish scaler – it's your ally in transforming your catch into a masterpiece.

Finally, let your fish rest after cooking. It's like allowing it to catch its breath before making its grand entrance onto your plate.

With these essential tools at your side and a dash of culinary confidence, you're well-equipped to conquer any recipe this cookbook throws your way. So, my culinary comrades, may your knives stay sharp, your pans stay hot, and your culinary creations be nothing short of magnificent. Anchors aweigh!

Maldivian Garudhiya
See page, 103

Flavor Pairing Suggestions

Ahoy, flavor adventurers! Prepare to embark on a gustatory expedition that's going to redefine the way you experience the sea's bounty. Here are some guiding stars, a treasure map of flavor pairings that'll awaken your inner chef and unleash your creative culinary spirit.

1. Citrus and Fresh Herbs: Imagine the zing of citrus meeting the aromatic embrace of fresh herbs. Lemon and dill dance harmoniously, while lime and cilantro tango with perfection. Whether it's a marinade, a dressing, or a finishing touch, this pairing is your passport to vibrant, refreshing dishes.

2. Spice and Smoke: Let's talk about the symphony of spice and smoke. Whether you're infusing your fish with a smoky essence or rubbing it with a fiery spice blend, the result is a marriage of complexity that ignites the senses. Think smoked paprika and cumin or a sprinkle of chipotle for that alluring heat.

3. Sweet and Savory: This is a balancing act that'll leave your taste buds in awe. Picture a delicate honey glaze on grilled fish, or a balsamic reduction drizzled over a seared fillet. The interplay of sweet and savory is a harmonious dance that can elevate your dishes to the realm of culinary artistry.

4. Tropical Fusion: Who can resist the allure of tropical flavors? Think mango and coconut, pineapple and ginger, or even a dash of passionfruit to elevate your fish to a sun-soaked paradise. It's a vacation for your palate, no passport required.

5. Mediterranean Medley: Let the Mediterranean breeze carry you away with a medley of olives, capers, tomatoes, and basil. This combination offers a symphony of tangy, earthy, and herbal notes that transport you to the sun-kissed shores of the Mediterranean.

6. Umami Symphony: Unleash the umami magic with ingredients like miso, soy sauce, and mushrooms. These umami powerhouses can transform your fish into an irresistible umami bomb, adding depth and richness to every bite.

7. Creamy Comfort: Embrace the comfort of creaminess with ingredients like butter, cream, and yogurt. A silky sauce can cradle your fish in a velvety embrace, creating a decadent symphony of textures and flavors.

8. Nutty Delights: Nuts bring a delightful crunch and a nutty undertone that can elevate your fish game. Try crushed almonds or pine nuts for that satisfying contrast in textures.

9. Wine and Vinegar: Elevate your cooking with the magic of wine and vinegar. A splash of white wine can add a touch of sophistication, while balsamic vinegar can introduce a delightful tanginess to your dish.

10. Pickled Piquancy: Experiment with pickled ingredients like red onions, jalapeños, or even pickled ginger. Their zesty kick can add a burst of excitement to your fish creations.

Now, my intrepid culinary explorers, take these flavor pairing suggestions and let your imagination run wild. Combine, experiment, and create your own culinary masterpieces that reflect your unique taste and style. Remember, the kitchen is your laboratory, and each dish you create is a canvas waiting to be painted with your flavor palette. So set sail on this flavor journey, and may your experiments be as bold as your appetite!

Chapter 1:
Grilled Delights

2 pieces

220 calories

30 minutes

Tandoori Fish Tikka

Ingredients:

- 1 lb firm white fish, cubed
- 2 tbsp tandoori masala
- 2 tbsp yogurt
- 1 tsp ginger-garlic paste
- 1 tsp red chili powder
- 1 tbsp lemon juice

An aromatic voyage to India. Marinated fish, charred to perfection. Vibrant spices dancing on your palate.

Directions

1. Mix masala, yogurt, paste, chili, lemon.
2. Marinate fish 20 min.
3. Skewer, grill till charred.
4. Serve with lemon wedges.

1 person

280
calories

20
minutes

Garlic-Herb Grilled Sea Bass

Ingredients:

- 1 sea bass fillet (8 oz)
- 3 cloves garlic, minced
- 2 tbsp fresh herbs (thyme, rosemary)
- 2 tbsp olive oil
- Salt and pepper

The Mediterranean whispers in every bite. Sea bass dressed in garlic and herbs, seared to golden elegance.

Directions

1. Preheat grill.
2. Mix garlic, herbs, oil, salt, pepper.
3. Rub mixture over fish.
4. Grill until flaky.
5. Savor the Mediterranean essence.

1 person

320
calories

30
minutes

Teriyaki Glazed Grilled Swordfish

Ingredients:

- 1 swordfish steak (8 oz)
- 3 tbsp teriyaki sauce
- 1 tbsp honey
- 1 tbsp soy sauce
- 1 tsp sesame oil
- 1 tsp ginger, grated

An East meets West delight. Swordfish basks in sweet teriyaki embrace, kissed by fire, a feast for the senses.

Directions

1. Mix teriyaki, honey, soy, sesame oil, ginger.
2. Marinate fish.
3. Grill 6-7 min each side.
4. Bask in the fusion flavors.

1 fillet

240
calories

25
minutes

Cajun Grilled Catfish

Ingredients:

- 2 catfish fillets (6 oz each)
- 2 tsp Cajun seasoning
- 1 tsp paprika
- 1 tsp thyme
- 1 tsp garlic powder
- Salt and pepper

Louisiana's soul on a plate. Catfish sings with Cajun spices, kissed by flames, soulful and spicy.

Directions

1. Preheat grill.
2. Mix Cajun seasoning, paprika, thyme, garlic, salt, pepper.
3. Coat fillets.
4. Grill until flaky.
5. Taste the Bayou.

1 fish

290
calories

35
minutes

Mediterranean
Grilled Branzino

Ingredients:

- 1 whole branzino (12 oz)
- 2 tbsp olive oil
- 2 cloves garlic, sliced
- 1 lemon, sliced
- Fresh herbs (thyme, oregano)
- Salt and pepper

A Greek symphony of flavors. Whole branzino, kissed by fire, drizzled with olive oil, an ode to the sea.

Directions

1. Preheat grill.
2. Rub fish with olive oil, garlic, herbs, salt, pepper.
3. Stuff lemon slices.
4. Grill 4-5 min each side.
5. Taste the Aegean.

1 person

280 calories

40 minutes

Thai Grilled Fish with Green Curry Marinade

Ingredients:

- 1 fish fillet (6 oz)
- 2 tbsp green curry paste
- 2 tbsp coconut milk
- 1 tbsp fish sauce
- 1 tbsp lime juice
- Fresh cilantro, chopped

A voyage to Thai shores. Fish marinated in green curry, grilled to perfection. A harmony of Thai flavors.

Directions

1. Mix curry paste, coconut milk, fish sauce, lime juice.
2. Marinate fish.
3. Grill until opaque.
4. Garnish with cilantro.
5. Taste Thailand.

1 steak

260
calories

25
minutes

Spicy Chipotle Grilled Mahi-Mahi

Ingredients:

- 1 mahi-mahi steak (8 oz)
- 2 tsp chipotle powder
- 1 tbsp olive oil
- 1 tbsp lime juice
- Salt and pepper

A fiesta of heat and flavor. Mahi-mahi kissed by chipotle spice, grilling to reveal smoky depth and zest.

Directions

1. Preheat grill.
2. Mix chipotle powder, olive oil, lime juice, salt, pepper.
3. Rub onto steak.
4. Grill 3-4 min each side.
5. Spice up your day.

2 steaks

300 calories

20 minutes

Soy-Ginger Grilled Tuna Steaks

Ingredients:

- 2 tuna steaks (6 oz each)
- 3 tbsp soy sauce
- 1 tbsp ginger, grated
- 1 tbsp sesame oil
- 1 tsp honey
- Green onions, sliced

An Asian fusion masterpiece. Tuna steaks marinated in soy-ginger goodness, kissed by the flames of perfection.

Directions

1. Mix soy sauce, ginger, sesame oil, honey.
2. Marinate steaks 10 min.
3. Grill 2-3 min each side.
4. Garnish with green onions.
5. Embrace fusion.

1 person

250
calories

30
minutes

Moroccan Spiced Grilled Snapper

Ingredients:

- 1 snapper fillet (6 oz)
- 2 tsp Moroccan spice blend
- 1 tbsp olive oil
- 1 lemon, sliced
- Fresh mint leaves
- Salt and pepper

An exotic North African affair. Snapper dances with Moroccan spices, charred to perfection. A taste of Marrakech.

Directions

1. Preheat grill.
2. Mix spice blend, olive oil, salt, pepper.
3. Coat fillet, place lemon slices.
4. Grill 4-5 min each side.
5. Journey to Morocco.

Chapter 2:
Classic Comforts

1
serving

550
calories

45
minutes

Fish and Chips
with Tartar Sauce

Ingredients:

- 1 cod fillet (6 oz)
- 1 cup potatoes, cut into strips
- 1 cup flour
- 1 tsp baking powder
- Salt and pepper
- Vegetable oil for frying
- Lemon wedges
- For tartar sauce: mayo, pickles, capers, herbs

A British love affair. Crispy fish, golden chips, tangy tartar sauce. Classic flavors, unrivaled in their comfort.

Directions

1. Heat oil to 350°F.
2. Dredge fish in seasoned flour.
3. Fry fish, then fries, until golden.
4. Serve with lemon wedges, tartar sauce.

Substitutions

Mayo for tartar sauce

1 bowl

380
calories

40
minutes

Creamy Seafood Chowder

Ingredients:

- 1 cup mixed seafood (shrimp, crab, clams)
- 2 tbsp butter
- 1 onion, diced
- 2 potatoes, diced
- 2 cups seafood or chicken broth
- 1 cup cream
- 1 bay leaf
- Fresh thyme
- Salt and pepper

A bowl of coastal comfort. Creamy chowder brimming with seafood treasures, warmth for the soul.

Directions

1. Sauté onion in butter. Add potatoes, broth, bay leaf, thyme, salt, pepper.
2. Simmer till tender.
3. Add seafood, cream.
4. Serve with warmth.

1 pie

450
calories

50
minutes

Traditional Fish Pie

Ingredients:

- 1 lb white fish fillets, cubed
- 1 cup mixed vegetables
- 2 tbsp butter
- 2 tbsp flour
- 1 cup milk
- Fresh parsley
- Puff pastry
- Egg wash (egg + milk)

A slice of British heritage. Flakey pastry hugs creamy fish filling. Comfort food that bridges generations.

Directions

1. Sauté vegetables in butter. Add flour, cook 2 min.
2. Stir in milk, cook till thickened.
3. Add fish, parsley.
4. Fill pastry-lined pie dish.
5. Bake golden.

1 plate

480 calories

35 minutes

Southern-Style Fish Fry

Ingredients:

- 2 catfish fillets (6 oz each)
- 1 cup cornmeal
- 1 tsp paprika
- 1 tsp garlic powder
- 1 tsp cayenne pepper
- Salt and pepper
- Vegetable oil for frying

A Southern tradition. Fish coated in seasoned cornmeal, fried to a golden symphony of crispiness.

Directions

1. Heat oil to 350°F.
2. Mix cornmeal, paprika, garlic powder, cayenne, salt, pepper.
3. Dredge fish, fry till crispy.
4. Savor Southern crunch.

1 fillet

420
calories

40
minutes

Beer-Battered Cod with Remoulade

Ingredients:

- 1 cod fillet (8 oz)
- 1 cup flour
- 1 tsp baking powder
- Salt and pepper
- 1 cup beer
- Vegetable oil for frying
- Lemon wedges
- For remoulade: mayo, pickles, capers, mustard

A pub classic. Cod dressed in beer-battered finery, served with remoulade for a tangy, zesty contrast.

Directions

1. Mix flour, baking powder, salt, pepper. Stir in beer.
2. Dredge fish, fry till golden.
3. Serve with lemon, remoulade.
4. Embrace the pub vibes.

Substitutions

Mustard for remoulade

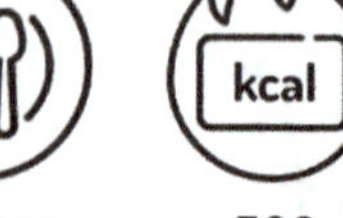

2 tacos

320 calories

30 minutes

Fish Tacos with Lime Crema

Ingredients:

- 1 lb white fish fillets
- 1 cup shredded cabbage
- 1 carrot, julienned
- Fresh cilantro
- Lime wedges
- For lime crema: sour cream, lime juice

A fiesta on a plate. Crispy fish, vibrant slaw, zesty lime crema, all wrapped in warm tortillas.

Directions

1. Mix cabbage, carrot, cilantro.
2. Dredge fish in flour, fry till crispy.
3. Mix sour cream, lime juice.
4. Assemble tacos, drizzle crema.
5. Fiesta time.

1 bowl

340 calories

50 minutes

New England Clam Chowder

Ingredients:

- 1 cup chopped clams
- 2 slices bacon, diced
- 1 onion, diced
- 2 potatoes, diced
- 2 cups clam juice
- 1 cup cream
- Fresh thyme
- Salt and pepper

A taste of coastal history. Creamy chowder laden with clams, potatoes, and nostalgia from the shores of New England.

Directions

1. Sauté bacon, onion. Add potatoes, clam juice, thyme, salt, pepper.
2. Simmer till potatoes are tender.
3. Add clams, cream.
4. Dive into tradition.

1 fillet

290
calories

20
minutes

Pan-Fried Perch with Garlic Butter

Ingredients:

- 2 perch fillets (4 oz each)
- 2 tbsp butter
- 2 cloves garlic, minced
- Fresh parsley
- Lemon wedges
- Salt and pepper

A lakeside delight. Perch fillet seared to golden perfection, adorned with a garlicky butter sauce.

Directions

1. Season fish with salt, pepper. Sear in butter.
2. Add garlic, cook briefly.
3. Drizzle with pan juices.
4. Plate with parsley, lemon.
5. Taste the lake.

1 bowl

380 calories

55 minutes

Italian Fish Stew (Cioppino)

Ingredients:

- 1 cup mixed seafood (clams, mussels, shrimp)
- 2 tbsp olive oil
- 1 onion, diced
- 2 cloves garlic, minced
- 1 can crushed tomatoes
- 1 cup white wine
- Fresh basil

A taste of Italy's coasts. Cioppino brimming with the bounty of the sea, a fragrant medley of seafood delights.

Directions

1. Sauté onion, garlic in oil. Add tomatoes, wine, simmer.
2. Add seafood, cook till shells open.
3. Garnish with basil.
4. Embrace Italian charm.

 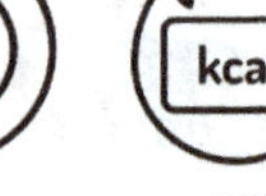 

1 pie

420
calories

60
minutes

Fisherman's Pie with Mashed Potatoes

Ingredients:

- 1 lb mixed white fish (cod, haddock), cubed
- 1 onion, diced
- 2 carrots, diced
- 1 cup frozen peas
- 2 tbsp butter
- 2 tbsp flour
- 1 cup milk
- Potatoes, butter, milk for mashed

A hearty tribute to seafaring souls. Flakey pie crowned with creamy mashed potatoes, a sea of flavors in every bite.

Directions

1. Sauté onion, carrots. Add flour, cook.
2. Stir in milk, fish, peas.
3. Fill pie dish.
4. Top with mashed potatoes.
5. Bake golden.
6. Sail away.

Chapter 3:
Asian Inspirations

1 person

340
calories

40
minutes

Thai Red Curry Fish

Ingredients:

- 1 fish fillet (6 oz)
- 2 tbsp red curry paste
- 1 cup coconut milk
- Thai basil leaves
- Kaffir lime leaves
- Fish sauce
- Palm sugar
- Lime juice

Substitutions

Thai holy basil for Thai basil

A voyage to Thailand's flavors. Fish swims in creamy red curry, a harmony of spice and silkiness.

Directions

1. Sauté curry paste.
2. Add coconut milk, leaves, seasonings.
3. Simmer, add fish.
4. Drizzle lime juice, serve with jasmine rice.
5. Taste Thailand.

1 fillet

360 calories

30 minutes

Japanese Miso-Glazed Black Cod

Ingredients:

- 1 black cod fillet (8 oz)
- 3 tbsp white miso paste
- 2 tbsp mirin
- 1 tbsp sake
- 1 tbsp sugar
- Vegetable oil for grilling

A taste of Japan's elegance. Black cod marinated in miso magic, grilled to succulent perfection.

Directions

1. Mix miso, mirin, sake, sugar.
2. Marinate fish.
3. Grill till caramelized.
4. Savor the umami symphony.

1 fish

320
calories

45
minutes

Korean Spicy Grilled Fish (Gui)

Ingredients:

- 1 whole fish (trout or mackerel)
- 3 tbsp gochujang
- 2 tbsp soy sauce
- 1 tbsp honey
- Sesame oil
- Minced garlic
- Sesame seeds
- Green onions

A taste of Korea's fire. Fish slathered in spicy gochujang glaze, grilled to smoky, spicy perfection.

Directions

1. Clean fish, score flesh.
2. Mix gochujang, soy sauce, honey, oil, garlic.
3. Rub onto fish.
4. Grill till charred.
5. Garnish, dive into Korea.

1 person **290 calories** **35 minutes**

Chinese Steamed Fish with Ginger and Scallions

Ingredients:

- 1 fish fillet (6 oz)
- 2 tbsp soy sauce
- 1 tbsp oyster sauce
- 1 tbsp ginger, julienned
- 2 scallions, sliced
- Sesame oil
- Fresh cilantro

A taste of China's delicate touch. Fish steamed with ginger, scallions, and soy, a harmonious dance of flavors.

Directions

1. Season fish with soy, oyster sauce, ginger.
2. Top with scallions.
3. Steam till opaque.
4. Drizzle with sesame oil, cilantro.
5. Taste China.

 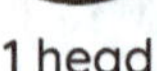  

1 head

380 calories

50 minutes

Malaysian Fish Head Curry

Ingredients:

- 1 fish head (snapper or grouper)
- 2 tbsp Malaysian curry paste
- 1 cup coconut milk
- Tamarind pulp
- Lemongrass
- Fresh herbs
- Vegetables

A bold journey into Malaysia's flavors. Fish head bathed in spicy coconut curry, a symphony of aroma and heat.

Directions

1. Sauté curry paste, add coconut milk, tamarind, lemongrass.
2. Simmer, add fish head, vegetables.
3. Garnish with herbs.
4. Dive into Malaysia.

1 bowl   400 calories   45 minutes

Indian Fish Curry (Meen Curry)

Ingredients:

- 1 lb fish fillets
- 2 tbsp Indian curry powder
- 1 onion, diced
- 2 tomatoes, chopped
- Coconut milk
- Tamarind pulp
- Fresh cilantro

A journey to India's heart. Fish curry with a burst of spices, a harmony of flavors that tell tales of the East.

Directions

1. Sauté onion, add curry powder, tomatoes.
2. Add coconut milk, tamarind, fish.
3. Simmer, garnish with cilantro.
4. Taste the spices of India.

1 fillet

340
calories

50
minutes

Vietnamese Caramelized Fish (Ca Kho)

Ingredients:

- 1 fish fillet (6 oz)
- 3 tbsp fish sauce
- 2 tbsp brown sugar
- Shallots, sliced
- Crushed black pepper
- Chilies
- Fresh herbs

A taste of Vietnam's depth. Fish caramelized in a clay pot, a sweet and savory symphony that tells tales of the South.

Directions

1. Mix fish sauce, sugar, shallots, pepper, chilies.
2. Caramelize sugar, add fish, cover.
3. Simmer till glazed.
4. Garnish with herbs.
5. Savor Vietnam.

1 fish

310
calories

40
minutes

Filipino Adobong Isda (Fish Adobo)

Ingredients:

- 1 whole fish (tilapia or mackerel)
- 1/4 cup soy sauce
- 1/4 cup vinegar
- 3 cloves garlic, minced
- Bay leaves
- Peppercorns
- Sugar

A taste of the Philippines. Fish adobo, marinated in soy-vinegar blend, simmered to tender perfection.

Directions

1. Marinate fish in soy, vinegar, garlic, bay, peppercorns.
2. Simmer till tender.
3. Serve with rice, savor the Philippines.

1 bowl   360 calories   55 minutes

Sri Lankan Fish Ambul Thiyal

Ingredients:

- 1 lb fish chunks
- 2 tbsp tamarind paste
- 2 tbsp Sri Lankan spice blend
- 1 cup coconut milk
- Curry leaves
- Pandan leaves
- Chili powder

A taste of Sri Lanka's zest. Fish ambul thiyal, slow-cooked with spices, tamarind, a symphony of sweet and sour.

Directions

1. Marinate fish in tamarind, spice blend, salt.
2. Sauté in coconut milk, add leaves, chili.
3. Simmer, taste the exotic spices of Sri Lanka.

1 fish

330
calories

50
minutes

Indonesian Spiced Grilled Fish (Ikan Bakar)

Ingredients:

- 1 whole fish (snapper or pomfret)
- 3 tbsp Indonesian spice blend
- Lime juice
- Kecap manis
- Lemongrass
- Turmeric leaves

A taste of Indonesia's fire. Fish marinated in fragrant spices, grilled over open flames, a dance of bold flavors.

Directions

1. Rub fish with spice blend, lime juice, kecap manis.
2. Grill with lemongrass, turmeric leaves.
3. Embrace the fiery spirit of Indonesia.

Chapter 4:
Fresh and Raw

1 person

350

15 mins

Classic Tuna Poke Bowl

Ingredients:

- 200g sushi-grade tuna, cubed
- 1/4 cup soy sauce
- 1 tbsp sesame oil
- 1 tsp grated ginger
- 1 tsp minced garlic
- 1 tsp sesame seeds
- 1/4 cup diced onion
- 1/4 cup chopped green onions
- 1 avocado, sliced
- 2 cups cooked white rice
- Nori seaweed, for garnish

The islands beckon with this Hawaiian staple.

Directions

1. In a bowl, mix soy sauce, sesame oil, ginger, garlic, and sesame seeds.
2. Add tuna, onion, and green onions. Toss gently.
3. Serve over rice.
4. Garnish with avocado and nori.
5. Feel the island breeze.

1 person

320

20 mins

Salmon Tartare with Avocado

Ingredients:

- 150g fresh salmon, finely chopped
- 1 avocado, diced
- 1 tbsp finely chopped red onion
- 1 tbsp capers, chopped
- 1 tbsp chopped fresh dill
- Zest and juice of 1 lemon
- Salt and pepper to taste

Elegance on a plate, a dance of textures and flavors.

Directions

1. Combine salmon, avocado, red onion, capers, and dill.
2. Add lemon zest and juice.
3. Season with salt and pepper.
4. Gently mix.
5. Serve with toasted crostini.
6. Indulge in the art of balance.

1 person | 280 | 25 mins

Ceviche Mixto

Ingredients:

- 150g mixed seafood (shrimp, squid, fish), diced
- 1/2 cup freshly squeezed lime juice
- 1/4 cup freshly squeezed lemon juice
- 1/4 cup diced red onion
- 1 rocoto pepper, finely chopped
- 2 tbsp chopped cilantro
- 1 sweet potato, boiled and sliced
- Corn, for garnish

Substitutions
Substitute rocoto

Peruvian pride, where the ocean's bounty meets tangy citrus.

Directions

1. Combine seafood, lime juice, and lemon juice. Let it "cook" for 20 mins.
2. Add onion, rocoto pepper, and cilantro.
3. Season to taste.
4. Serve with sweet potato and corn.
5. Taste the tang of tradition.

1 person | 240 | 10 mins

Sashimi Platter with Wasabi and Soy Sauce

Ingredients:

- Assorted sashimi (tuna, salmon, yellowtail)
- Wasabi
- Soy sauce
- Pickled ginger

The Japanese artistry, pristine slices dipped in harmony.

Directions

1. Arrange sashimi on a platter.
2. Serve with wasabi, soy sauce, and pickled ginger.
3. Delve into the simplicity of perfection.

1 person | 180 | 15 mins

Mediterranean Tuna Carpaccio

Ingredients:

- 150g fresh tuna, thinly sliced
- 1/4 cup extra-virgin olive oil
- 1 tbsp lemon juice
- 1 tsp capers
- 1 tsp chopped fresh parsley
- Salt and pepper to taste

Sun-soaked flavors of the Mediterranean dance on your palate.

Directions

1. Arrange tuna slices on a plate.
2. Drizzle olive oil and lemon juice.
3. Sprinkle capers and parsley.
4. Season with salt and pepper.
5. Bask in the Mediterranean sun.

1 person   310   20 mins

Hawaiian Ahi Poke

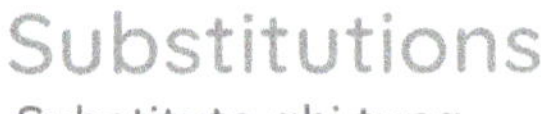

Ingredients:

- 200g ahi tuna, cubed
- 1/4 cup soy sauce
- 1 tsp sesame oil
- 1 tsp rice vinegar
- 1 tsp minced ginger
- 1/4 cup chopped green onions
- 1/2 tsp red pepper flakes
- 1 tsp toasted sesame seeds
- 1 cup sushi rice
- Pineapple chunks, for garnish

Substitutions
Substitute ahi tuna

Aloha spirit in a bowl, a taste of the Pacific waves.

Directions

1. Mix tuna, soy sauce, sesame oil, rice vinegar, and ginger.
2. Add green onions and red pepper flakes.
3. Top with sesame seeds.
4. Serve over sushi rice.
5. Garnish with pineapple.
6. Embrace the spirit of Hawaii.

1 person | 260 | 30 mins

Seared Scallops with Mango Salsa

Ingredients:

- 4 large scallops
- Salt and pepper to taste
- 1 tbsp olive oil
- 1 ripe mango, diced
- 1/4 cup diced red bell pepper
- 2 tbsp chopped red onion
- 1 small jalapeno, minced
- 2 tbsp chopped cilantro
- Juice of 1 lime
- Mixed greens, for serving

Seared elegance meets tropical vibrancy, a dance of land and sea.

Directions

1. Season scallops with salt and pepper.
2. Heat oil in a skillet; sear scallops.
3. Combine mango, red bell pepper, red onion, jalapeno, and cilantro.
4. Add lime juice.
5. Serve scallops on mixed greens.
6. Relish the dance of flavors.

Substitutions
Substitute scallops

1 person   280   25 mins

Smoked Salmon and Cream Cheese Sushi Rolls

Ingredients:

- 2 nori sheets
- 1 cup sushi rice
- 2 oz smoked salmon
- 2 oz cream cheese
- Cucumber sticks
- Avocado slices
- Soy sauce
- Wasabi
- Pickled ginger

East meets West in a delicate embrace of smoky indulgence.

Directions

1. Place nori on a bamboo mat.
2. Spread rice over nori; leave a border.
3. Lay smoked salmon, cream cheese, cucumber, and avocado.
4. Roll tightly.
5. Slice and serve with soy sauce, wasabi, and pickled ginger.
6. Celebrate the fusion of flavors.

1 person   220   30 mins

Thai Fish Larb Lettuce Wraps

Ingredients:

- 150g white fish fillet, minced
- 2 tbsp fish sauce
- 2 tbsp lime juice
- 1 tbsp roasted rice powder
- 1/4 cup chopped mint leaves
- 1/4 cup chopped cilantro
- 2 tbsp chopped shallots
- Lettuce leaves, for wrapping

Substitutions

Substitute white fish

A harmonious melody of Thai spices, a journey for the palate.

Directions

1. Cook fish; mix with fish sauce, lime juice, and rice powder.
2. Add mint, cilantro, and shallots.
3. Spoon into lettuce leaves.
4. Revel in the Thai symphony.
5. Crunch and savor the experience.

1 person   260   25 mins

Peruvian Tiradito with Aji Amarillo Sauce

Ingredients:

- 150g white fish, thinly sliced
- 1/4 cup aji amarillo sauce
- 2 tbsp freshly squeezed lime juice
- 1 tsp minced garlic
- 1 tsp chopped cilantro
- 1/2 tsp red pepper flakes
- 1 sweet potato, boiled and sliced
- Cancha corn, for garnish

A Peruvian masterpiece, where the canvas is fish and the brush is fire.

Directions

1. Arrange fish on a plate.
2. Drizzle aji amarillo sauce and lime juice.
3. Sprinkle garlic, cilantro, and red pepper flakes.
4. Serve with sweet potato and cancha corn.
5. Feel the Peruvian fire in every bite.

Chapter 5:
Baked Brilliance

1 person | 280 | 25 mins

Baked Herb-Crusted Cod

Ingredients:

- 1 cod fillet
- 2 tbsp breadcrumbs
- 1 tbsp chopped fresh herbs (rosemary, thyme, parsley)
- 1 tbsp olive oil
- Salt and pepper to taste

A crispy herb embrace for the mighty cod.

Directions

1. Preheat oven.
2. Mix breadcrumbs, herbs, olive oil, salt, and pepper.
3. Coat cod with mixture.
4. Bake until golden and cooked through.
5. Serve with a squeeze of lemon.
6. Revel in the herbaceous symphony.

1 person 250 30 mins

Lemon-Baked Tilapia with Garlic Butter

Ingredients:

- 1 tilapia fillet
- 2 tbsp melted butter
- Juice and zest of 1 lemon
- 2 garlic cloves, minced
- Fresh thyme
- Salt and pepper to taste

Tilapia dances in lemony-garlic ecstasy.

Directions

1. Preheat oven.
2. Lay tilapia on foil.
3. Mix butter, lemon juice and zest, garlic, thyme, salt, and pepper.
4. Drizzle over tilapia.
5. Seal foil and bake.
6. Unveil the zesty surprise.

1 person | 320 | 40 mins

Italian Stuffed Branzino

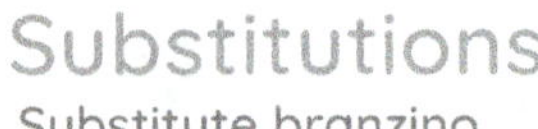

Ingredients:

- 1 branzino, cleaned and scaled
- 1/4 cup breadcrumbs
- 2 tbsp chopped fresh herbs (parsley, oregano, thyme)
- 1 lemon, sliced
- 2 garlic cloves, minced
- Olive oil
- Salt and pepper to taste

Substitutions
Substitute branzino

Branzino, a canvas for a medley of Italian flavors.

Directions

1. Preheat oven.
2. Mix breadcrumbs, herbs, lemon zest, garlic, salt, and pepper.
3. Stuff branzino with mixture and lemon slices.
4. Drizzle with olive oil.
5. Bake until fish flakes.
6. Immerse in Italian aromas.

1 person   290   35 mins

Greek Baked Fish with Tomatoes and Olives

Sun-soaked Greece on your plate.

Ingredients:

- 1 fish fillet (sea bream, sea bass)
- 1 cup cherry tomatoes, halved
- 1/4 cup Kalamata olives
- 1/4 cup feta cheese, crumbled
- Fresh oregano
- Olive oil
- Salt and pepper to taste

Directions

1. Preheat oven.
2. Lay fish on a bed of cherry tomatoes and olives.
3. Drizzle olive oil; season with oregano, salt, and pepper.
4. Bake until fish is cooked.
5. Crumble feta over the top.
6. Close your eyes and feel the Aegean breeze.

Substitutions
Substitute fish fillet

1 person   **350**   **40 mins**

Creamy Baked Salmon with Spinach and Feta

Salmon swathed in a cloak of creamy indulgence.

Ingredients:

- 1 salmon fillet
- 1/4 cup heavy cream
- 1/4 cup crumbled feta cheese
- 1 cup baby spinach
- 1 lemon, sliced
- Fresh dill
- Salt and pepper to taste

Directions

1. Preheat oven.
2. Lay salmon on foil.
3. Mix cream, feta, spinach, lemon zest, dill, salt, and pepper.
4. Pour over salmon.
5. Top with lemon slices.
6. Bake until salmon is flaky.
7. Immerse in the creaminess.

1 person   270   30 mins

Provençal Baked
Sea Bass

Ingredients:

- 1 sea bass fillet
- 1/4 cup chopped tomatoes
- 1/4 cup chopped red bell pepper
- 1/4 cup chopped red onion
- 2 garlic cloves, minced
- Fresh thyme
- Olive oil
- Salt and pepper to taste

A Provençal voyage on a sea bass canvas.

Directions

1. Preheat oven.
2. Place sea bass on a bed of tomatoes, bell pepper, and onion.
3. Sprinkle garlic, thyme, salt, and pepper.
4. Drizzle with olive oil.
5. Bake until fish is tender.
6. Let the Provençal sun shine through.

1 person | 300 | 45 mins

Coconut-Curry Baked Red Snapper

A symphony of coconut and curry to tickle your taste buds.

Ingredients:

- 1 red snapper fillet
- 1/4 cup coconut milk
- 2 tbsp red curry paste
- 1 tbsp fish sauce
- 1 tbsp brown sugar
- Lime wedges
- Fresh cilantro
- Salt to taste

Directions

1. Preheat oven.
2. Mix coconut milk, curry paste, fish sauce, and brown sugar.
3. Lay snapper on foil.
4. Pour coconut-curry mixture over fish.
5. Sprinkle with salt.
6. Bake until fish is cooked.
7. Squeeze lime; garnish with cilantro.
8. Delight in the curry crescendo.

1 person | 320 | 50 mins

Moroccan Baked Fish with Charmoula Sauce

Ingredients:

- 1 fish fillet (cod, haddock)
- 1/4 cup charmoula sauce
- 1 lemon, sliced
- Fresh cilantro
- Olive oil
- Salt and pepper to taste

A Moroccan tale of spices and charmoula.

Directions

1. Preheat oven.
2. Lay fish on foil.
3. Spread charmoula sauce over fish.
4. Top with lemon slices.
5. Drizzle with olive oil; season.
6. Bake until fish is flaky.
7. Garnish with cilantro.
8. Embark on a culinary journey to Morocco.

Substitutions

Substitute fish fillet

1 person   340   40 mins

Pesto-Stuffed Baked Trout

Ingredients:

- 1 trout, gutted and cleaned
- 2 tbsp pesto
- 1 lemon, sliced
- Fresh basil leaves
- Olive oil
- Salt and pepper to taste

Trout, a vessel for a delightful pesto surprise.

Directions

1. Preheat oven.
2. Stuff trout with pesto and lemon slices.
3. Drizzle with olive oil; season.
4. Bake until fish is cooked.
5. Garnish with basil leaves.
6. Unveil the pesto treasure.

1 person   360   35 mins

Parmesan-Crusted Baked Halibut

Ingredients:

- 1 halibut fillet
- 2 tbsp grated parmesan cheese
- 2 tbsp breadcrumbs
- 1 tbsp melted butter
- Lemon zest
- Fresh parsley
- Salt and pepper to taste

Substitutions

-

Halibut, a canvas for a golden parmesan crust.

Directions

1. Preheat oven.
2. Lay halibut on foil.
3. Mix parmesan, breadcrumbs, melted butter, lemon zest, salt, and pepper.
4. Press mixture onto halibut.
5. Bake until crust is golden.
6. Garnish with parsley.
7. Savor the harmonious contrast.

We need your support

Hey, fellow food explorers! Before we dive into this flavor-packed journey, I've got a quick favor to ask.

Could you spare a minute? If you're up for it, consider leaving a quick review. Your words are like culinary gold for us – they're hard to come by, and they make a world of difference.

We're a small crew, and your reviews help us more than you can imagine. So, if you've got a sec, head over to where you got this book and drop a rating and a sentence. We read and appreciate every single one.

Okay, back to the good stuff – the recipes are waiting! Thanks for being here, and let's dig into the deliciousness together.

Chapter 6:
Exotic Flavors

1 person   380   50 mins

Brazilian Moqueca (Fish Stew)

Ingredients:

- 1 fish fillet (snapper, grouper)
- 1/2 cup coconut milk
- 1/4 cup diced tomatoes
- 1/4 cup diced bell peppers
- 1/4 cup diced onion
- 2 garlic cloves, minced
- 1 tbsp palm oil
- Lime wedges
- Fresh cilantro
- Salt and pepper to taste

Substitutions
Substitute palm oil

A rich Brazilian tale told through fish and coconut.

Directions

1. Preheat oven.
2. Lay fish on a bed of tomatoes, bell peppers, and onions.
3. Mix garlic, palm oil, salt, and pepper.
4. Pour coconut milk over fish.
5. Seal with foil and bake.
6. Unveil the Brazilian harmony.
7. Serve with lime and cilantro.

1 person | 320 | 45 mins

Peruvian Causa Rellena de Atún

Ingredients:

- 1 large potato, boiled and mashed
- 1 can tuna, drained
- 1/4 cup mayonnaise
- 1 tbsp ají amarillo paste
- 1 tbsp lime juice
- Fresh cilantro
- Salt and pepper to taste

Substitutions
Substitute ají amarillo paste

Peruvian artistry, where tuna meets potato in a melody.

Directions

1. Mix tuna, mayonnaise, ají amarillo paste, lime juice, salt, and pepper.
2. Spread half of mashed potato in a dish.
3. Layer tuna mixture.
4. Top with remaining potato.
5. Garnish with cilantro.
6. Revel in the Peruvian melody.

1 person   340   50 mins

Mexican Fish Veracruzana

Ingredients:

- 1 fish fillet (red snapper, tilapia)
- 1/4 cup tomato sauce
- 1/4 cup diced tomatoes
- 2 tbsp sliced green olives
- 1 tbsp capers
- 1/4 cup diced onion
- 2 garlic cloves, minced
- Jalapeño slices
- Fresh cilantro
- Olive oil
- Salt and pepper to taste

Substitutions
Substitute fish fillet

A Mexican symphony of tomatoes, olives, and capers.

Directions
1. Preheat oven.
2. Lay fish on foil.
3. Mix tomato sauce, tomatoes, olives, capers, onion, garlic, jalapeño, salt, and pepper.
4. Pour mixture over fish.
5. Drizzle with olive oil.
6. Seal foil and bake.
7. Garnish with cilantro.
8. Dance to the Mexican rhythm.

1 person | 360 | 55 mins

Lebanese Samke Harra (Spicy Fish)

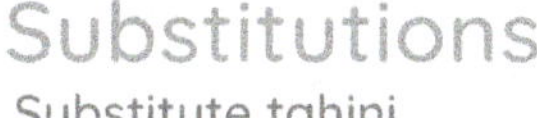

Ingredients:

- 1 fish fillet (tilapia, bass)
- 1/4 cup tahini
- 2 tbsp lemon juice
- 1/4 cup chopped walnuts
- 2 garlic cloves, minced
- 1 tbsp olive oil
- Chili flakes
- Fresh parsley
- Salt and pepper to taste

Substitutions
Substitute tahini

Lebanese magic, where fish meets a fiery chili embrace.

Directions

1. Preheat oven.
2. Lay fish on foil.
3. Mix tahini, lemon juice, garlic, olive oil, chili flakes, salt, and pepper.
4. Spread mixture over fish.
5. Sprinkle chopped walnuts.
6. Bake until fish is cooked.
7. Garnish with parsley.
8. Embrace the Lebanese fire.

1 person

410

60 mins

Russian Fish Kulebyaka (Salmon Pie)

Ingredients:

- 1 salmon fillet
- 1/2 cup cooked rice
- 1/4 cup sliced mushrooms
- 1/4 cup chopped onion
- 2 hard-boiled eggs, sliced
- Fresh dill
- Puff pastry
- Egg wash
- Salt and pepper to taste

A Russian tale told through a flaky salmon pie.

Directions

1. Preheat oven.
2. Layer rice, mushrooms, onion, eggs, and dill.
3. Lay salmon on top.
4. Season with salt and pepper.
5. Encase in puff pastry.
6. Brush with egg wash.
7. Bake until golden.
8. Unveil the Russian tradition.

1 person | 330 | 45 mins

Thai Pla Rad Prik (Crispy Fish with Chili Sauce)

Ingredients:

- 1 fish fillet (sea bass, catfish)
- 2 tbsp cornstarch
- 2 tbsp fish sauce
- 1 tbsp oyster sauce
- 1 tbsp sugar
- 2 garlic cloves, minced
- Fresh Thai chilies
- Fresh cilantro
- Lime wedges

Substitutions
Substitute fish fillet

Thai crescendo, crispy fish serenaded by chili sauce.

Directions

1. Preheat oven.
2. Coat fish with cornstarch.
3. Bake until crispy.
4. Mix fish sauce, oyster sauce, sugar, garlic, and chilies.
5. Drizzle sauce over fish.
6. Garnish with cilantro and lime.
7. Let the Thai notes enthrall you.

1 person   290   50 mins

Spanish Bacalao a la Vizcaína (Cod in Tomato Sauce)

Ingredients:

- 1 cod fillet
- 1/4 cup tomato sauce
- 1/4 cup diced bell peppers
- 1/4 cup diced onion
- 2 garlic cloves, minced
- Paprika
- Olive oil
- Salt and pepper to taste

Substitutions
Substitute cod fillet

Spanish romance, cod swathed in tomato embrace.

Directions

1. Preheat oven.
2. Lay cod on foil.
3. Mix tomato sauce, bell peppers, onion, garlic, paprika, salt, and pepper.
4. Spread mixture over cod.
5. Drizzle with olive oil.
6. Bake until cod is flaky.
7. Revel in the Spanish passion.

1 person | 350 | 55 mins

Nigerian Fish Pepper Soup

Ingredients:

- 1 fish fillet (tilapia, catfish)
- 1/4 cup blended pepper mix
- 1/4 cup sliced onions
- 2 garlic cloves, minced
- 1 tsp ground crayfish
- Fresh basil leaves
- Stock cubes
- Salt and pepper to taste

Substitutions
Substitute fish fillet

Nigerian soul, where fish meets a peppery hug.

Directions

1. Preheat oven.
2. Lay fish on foil.
3. Mix pepper mix, onions, garlic, crayfish, stock cubes, salt, and pepper.
4. Pour mixture over fish.
5. Seal foil and bake.
6. Garnish with basil leaves.
7. Embrace the Nigerian warmth.

1 person

330

60 mins

Jamaican Escovitch Fish

Ingredients:

- 1 fish fillet (snapper, parrotfish)
- 1/4 cup sliced onions
- 1/4 cup sliced bell peppers
- 2 Scotch bonnet peppers, sliced
- 1 carrot, julienned
- 1 cup vinegar
- Pimento berries
- Salt and pepper to taste

Substitutions
Substitute fish fillet

Jamaican melody, where fish sings with a pickled tang.

Directions

1. Preheat oven.
2. Lay fish on foil.
3. Mix onions, bell peppers, Scotch bonnet peppers, carrot, vinegar, pimento, salt, and pepper.
4. Pour mixture over fish.
5. Seal foil and bake.
6. Relish the Jamaican medley.

1 person   290   40 mins

Korean Fish Jeon (Fish Pancakes)

Korean dance of flavors, fish pancakes in crispy embrace.

Ingredients:

- 1 fish fillet (mackerel, pollack)
- 1/4 cup all-purpose flour
- 2 tbsp chopped scallions
- 1 egg
- Soy sauce
- Sesame oil
- Salt and pepper to taste

Directions

1. Preheat oven.
2. Coat fish with flour.
3. Dip in egg wash; coat with flour again.
4. Bake until crispy.
5. Mix soy sauce, sesame oil, scallions, salt, and pepper.
6. Dip pancakes in sauce.
7. Immerse in Korean delights.

Substitutions
Substitute fish fillet

Chapter 7:
Seafood Fusion

1 person   360   40 mins

Blackened Fish Tacos with Mango Salsa

Ingredients:

- 1 fish fillet (tilapia, snapper)
- 2 tbsp blackened seasoning
- 2 soft taco shells
- 1/4 cup diced mango
- 1/4 cup diced red onion
- 1/4 cup chopped cilantro
- Lime wedges
- Greek yogurt
- Salt and pepper to taste

Substitutions
Substitute fish fillet

A fiesta of flavors, where tacos meet the tropics.

Directions

1. Preheat oven.
2. Coat fish with blackened seasoning.
3. Bake until fish is cooked.
4. Flake fish; stuff taco shells.
5. Mix mango, red onion, cilantro, salt, and pepper.
6. Top tacos with mango salsa.
7. Drizzle with Greek yogurt.
8. Squeeze lime; embrace the fiesta.

1 person   390   55 mins

Mediterranean Seafood Paella

Ingredients:

- 1/2 cup arborio rice
- 1/4 cup mixed seafood (shrimp, mussels, calamari)
- 1/4 cup diced bell peppers
- 1/4 cup diced tomatoes
- 1/4 cup diced onion
- 2 garlic cloves, minced
- Saffron threads
- Fresh parsley
- Lemon wedges
- Olive oil
- Salt and pepper to taste

Substitutions
Substitute arborio rice

Paella with a coastal twist, a journey through the Mediterranean.

Directions

1. Preheat oven.
2. Cook rice until al dente.
3. Sauté seafood, bell peppers, tomatoes, onion, and garlic.
4. Mix rice and sautéed mixture.
5. Add saffron threads.
6. Bake until paella is golden.
7. Garnish with parsley.
8. Serve with lemon wedges.
9. Revel in the Mediterranean melody.

1 person | 380 | 50 mins

Thai Green Curry Seafood

Ingredients:

- 1 fish fillet (cod, shrimp)
- 1/4 cup Thai green curry paste
- 1/4 cup coconut milk
- 1/4 cup diced bell peppers
- 1/4 cup diced zucchini
- 1/4 cup sliced bamboo shoots
- Fresh Thai basil
- Lime wedges
- Jasmine rice
- Salt and pepper to taste

Substitutions
Substitute Thai green curry paste

Thai green curry meets a symphony of seafood.

Directions

1. Preheat oven.
2. Coat fish with green curry paste.
3. Bake until fish is cooked.
4. Sauté bell peppers, zucchini, and bamboo shoots.
5. Add coconut milk; simmer.
6. Top curry with fish.
7. Garnish with Thai basil.
8. Serve with lime wedges and jasmine rice.
9. Let the Thai flavors dance.

1 person | 350 | 60 mins

Caribbean Seafood Roti

Ingredients:

- 1 fish fillet (kingfish, snapper)
- 1/4 cup diced potatoes
- 1/4 cup diced carrots
- 1/4 cup diced bell peppers
- 1/4 cup diced onion
- 2 garlic cloves, minced
- 1 tbsp curry powder
- Roti bread
- Fresh cilantro
- Hot pepper sauce
- Salt and pepper to taste

Substitutions
Substitute fish fillet

Caribbean delight, seafood wrapped in flaky roti.

Directions

1. Preheat oven.
2. Sauté potatoes, carrots, bell peppers, onion, and garlic.
3. Add curry powder.
4. Bake fish until cooked.
5. Flake fish; mix with sautéed vegetables.
6. Warm roti bread.
7. Stuff with seafood mixture.
8. Garnish with cilantro.
9. Add hot pepper sauce for a Caribbean kick.
10. Embrace the island breeze.

1 person | 370 | 45 mins

Sushi Burrito with Spicy Mayo

Ingredients:

- 1 fish fillet (salmon, tuna)
- 1/2 cup sushi rice
- 1 nori sheet
- 1/4 cup sliced cucumber
- 1/4 cup sliced avocado
- 1/4 cup julienned carrots
- Spicy mayo
- Soy sauce
- Sesame seeds
- Salt and pepper to taste

Substitutions
Substitute fish fillet

Sushi meets burrito, a roll of fusion perfection.

Directions

1. Preheat oven.
2. Bake fish until done.
3. Season rice; spread on nori sheet.
4. Lay fish, cucumber, avocado, and carrots.
5. Drizzle with spicy mayo.
6. Roll tightly; slice.
7. Serve with soy sauce and sesame seeds.
8. Relish the sushi-burrito dance.

1 person   380   60 mins

Seafood Gumbo

A Louisiana story, where seafood swims in a gumbo sea.

Ingredients:

- 1/4 cup shrimp
- 1/4 cup crab meat
- 1/4 cup diced bell peppers
- 1/4 cup diced celery
- 1/4 cup diced onion
- 2 garlic cloves, minced
- 1/4 cup diced tomatoes
- 1/4 cup okra slices
- 1/4 cup andouille sausage, sliced
- Chicken or seafood broth
- Cajun seasoning
- Fresh parsley
- Rice
- Salt and pepper to taste

Substitutions

Substitute andouille sausage

Directions

1. Preheat oven.
2. Sauté shrimp, crab, bell peppers, celery, onion, and garlic.
3. Add tomatoes, okra, sausage, broth, and Cajun seasoning.
4. Simmer.
5. Serve over rice; garnish with parsley.
6. Immerse in the gumbo symphony.
7. Cajun dreams come true.

1 person   360   50 mins

Cajun Seafood Pasta

Ingredients:

- 1/2 cup linguine pasta
- 1/4 cup shrimp
- 1/4 cup diced bell peppers
- 1/4 cup diced onion
- 1/4 cup sliced mushrooms
- 2 garlic cloves, minced
- 1/4 cup heavy cream
- Cajun seasoning
- Fresh parsley
- Olive oil
- Salt and pepper to taste

Substitutions
Substitute linguine pasta

Cajun magic, where pasta meets a symphony of seafood.

Directions

1. Preheat oven.
2. Cook pasta until al dente.
3. Sauté shrimp, bell peppers, onion, mushrooms, and garlic.
4. Add heavy cream and Cajun seasoning.
5. Toss in pasta; drizzle with olive oil.
6. Garnish with parsley.
7. Let the Cajun flavors dance on your palate.

1 person | 390 | 60 mins

Seafood Risotto with Saffron

A saffron-kissed journey, where seafood luxuriates in risotto.

Ingredients:

- 1/2 cup Arborio rice
- 1/4 cup mixed seafood (shrimp, scallops)
- 1/4 cup diced bell peppers
- 1/4 cup diced onion
- 2 garlic cloves, minced
- Saffron threads
- White wine
- Chicken or seafood broth
- Fresh parsley
- Parmesan cheese
- Salt and pepper to taste

Directions

1. Preheat oven.
2. Sauté seafood, bell peppers, onion, and garlic.
3. Toast Arborio rice.
4. Add saffron threads and white wine.
5. Gradually add broth; stir until creamy.
6. Mix in seafood mixture.
7. Garnish with parsley and Parmesan.
8. Delight in the saffron symphony.

Substitutions

Substitute Arborio rice

1 person   350   45 mins

Mexican Seafood Ceviche Tostadas

Ingredients:

- 1/4 cup mixed seafood (shrimp, fish)
- 1/4 cup diced tomatoes
- 1/4 cup diced red onion
- 1/4 cup diced cucumber
- 1/4 cup diced avocado
- 1/4 cup chopped cilantro
- Lime juice
- Jalapeño slices
- Tostada shells
- Salt and pepper to taste

Substitutions
Substitute mixed seafood

Mexican coastal bliss, ceviche atop crispy tostadas.

Directions

1. Preheat oven.
2. Mix seafood, tomatoes, red onion, cucumber, avocado, and cilantro.
3. Squeeze lime juice; season with salt and pepper.
4. Spoon ceviche onto tostada shells.
5. Top with jalapeño slices.
6. Savor the Mexican coastal breeze.
7. Let the fiesta begin.

1 person   370   50 mins

Asian Seafood Noodle Stir-Fry

Ingredients:

- 1/4 cup mixed seafood (shrimp, squid)
- 1/2 cup cooked Asian noodles
- 1/4 cup sliced bell peppers
- 1/4 cup sliced mushrooms
- 1/4 cup sliced snow peas
- 1/4 cup diced onion
- 2 garlic cloves, minced
- Soy sauce
- Sesame oil
- Fresh cilantro
- Lime wedges
- Salt and pepper to taste

Substitutions
Substitute mixed seafood

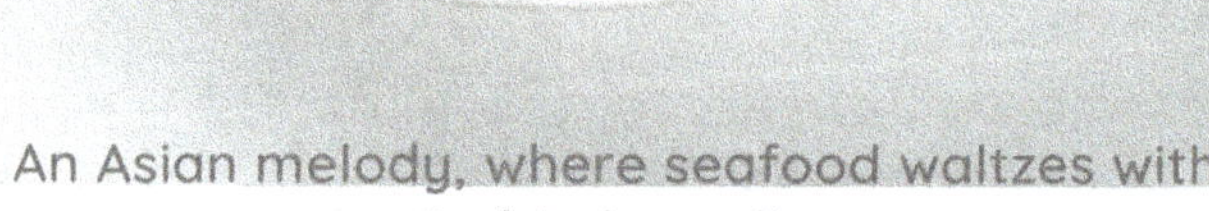

An Asian melody, where seafood waltzes with stir-fried noodles.

Directions

1. Preheat oven.
2. Sauté seafood, bell peppers, mushrooms, snow peas, and onion.
3. Add cooked noodles.
4. Drizzle with soy sauce and sesame oil.
5. Garnish with cilantro.
6. Serve with lime wedges.
7. Savor the Asian dance of flavors.
8. Embark on an Eastern journey.

Chapter 8:
Elegant Entrees

1 person   450   75 mins

Lobster Thermidor

A luxurious classic, lobster crowned with creamy glory.

Ingredients:

- 1 lobster tail
- 1/4 cup diced mushrooms
- 1/4 cup diced shallots
- 1/4 cup white wine
- 1/4 cup heavy cream
- 1/4 cup grated Gruyère cheese
- Fresh tarragon
- Dijon mustard
- Lemon juice
- Salt and pepper to taste

Directions

1. Preheat oven.
2. Sauté mushrooms and shallots.
3. Add wine; reduce.
4. Stir in cream, cheese, tarragon, mustard, lemon juice, salt, and pepper.
5. Broil lobster; top with sauce.
6. Embrace the creamy elegance.
7. Savor the indulgence.

Substitutions

Substitute Gruyère cheese

1 person | 320 | 40 mins

Seared Scallops with Truffle Oil

Ingredients:

- 4 large scallops
- 1 tbsp truffle oil
- 1/4 cup white wine
- 2 tbsp butter
- Fresh chives
- Lemon zest
- Salt and pepper to taste

Substitutions

Substitute truffle oil

Seared scallops dance with truffle oil in this opulent dish.

Directions

1. Preheat oven.
2. Sear scallops until golden.
3. Drizzle with truffle oil.
4. Deglaze with white wine; add butter.
5. Season with chives, lemon zest, salt, and pepper.
6. Revel in the truffle symphony.
7. A taste of elegance awaits.

1 person | 380 | 50 mins

Pan-Roasted Monkfish with Brown Butter

Ingredients:

- 1 monkfish fillet
- 2 tbsp butter
- 1/4 cup chopped shallots
- 2 garlic cloves, minced
- Fresh thyme
- Lemon juice
- White wine
- Salt and pepper to taste

Substitutions
Substitute monkfish

Monkfish takes center stage, adorned with luscious brown butter.

Directions

1. Preheat oven.
2. Sear monkfish until golden.
3. Add butter; cook until browned.
4. Sauté shallots and garlic; deglaze with wine.
5. Finish with thyme, lemon juice, salt, and pepper.
6. Drizzle brown butter over monkfish.
7. A symphony of flavors awaits.
8. Savor the elegance.

1 person   420   60 mins

Chilean Sea Bass with Champagne Sauce

Ingredients:

- 1 sea bass fillet
- 1/4 cup champagne
- 1/4 cup heavy cream
- 1/4 cup diced shallots
- 1/4 cup diced mushrooms
- Fresh dill
- Lemon zest
- Salt and pepper to taste

Substitutions
Substitute champagne

Chilean sea bass, a canvas for a champagne-infused sauce.

Directions

1. Preheat oven.
2. Sear sea bass; remove.
3. Sauté shallots and mushrooms.
4. Add champagne; reduce.
5. Pour in cream; simmer.
6. Finish with dill, lemon zest, salt, and pepper.
7. Pour champagne sauce over sea bass.
8. Indulge in the champagne dream.
9. Elevate your senses.

1 person   380   45 mins

King Crab Legs with Garlic Butter

King crab legs drenched in golden garlic butter.

Ingredients:

- 2 king crab legs
- 4 tbsp melted butter
- 2 garlic cloves, minced
- Fresh parsley
- Lemon wedges
- Salt and pepper to taste

Directions

1. Preheat oven.
2. Split crab legs; crack shells slightly.
3. Mix melted butter and garlic.
4. Brush crab legs with garlic butter.
5. Bake until crab is heated.
6. Garnish with parsley and lemon wedges.
7. Succumb to the crab indulgence.
8. Unveil the king's feast.

Substitutions

Substitute king crab legs

1 person

330

50 mins

Grilled Whole Red Snapper with Herbs

Ingredients:

- 1 whole red snapper
- 2 tbsp olive oil
- Fresh herbs (rosemary, thyme)
- Lemon slices
- Salt and pepper to taste

A showstopper, red snapper grilled to perfection with herbaceous charm.

Directions

1. Preheat oven.
2. Rub snapper with olive oil; season inside and out.
3. Stuff cavity with herbs and lemon slices.
4. Grill snapper until flesh is flaky.
5. Embrace the herb-infused delight.
6. Savor the seafood spectacle.

Substitutions

Substitute red snapper

1 person • 340 • 60 mins

Oysters Rockefeller

Ingredients:

- 4 fresh oysters
- 1/4 cup chopped spinach
- 1/4 cup diced onions
- 1/4 cup diced celery
- 1/4 cup breadcrumbs
- 1/4 cup grated Parmesan cheese
- Anise liqueur
- Fresh parsley
- Salt and pepper to taste

Substitutions
Substitute anise liqueur

Oysters transformed, crowned with spinach and elegance.

Directions

1. Preheat oven.
2. Sauté onions and celery; add spinach.
3. Mix breadcrumbs, Parmesan, liqueur, salt, and pepper.
4. Top oysters with spinach mixture.
5. Bake until oysters are cooked.
6. Garnish with parsley.
7. Savor the oyster transformation.
8. Elegance on the half shell.

1 person | 360 | 40 mins

Pan-Seared Halibut with Lemon-Caper Sauce

Ingredients:

- 1 halibut fillet
- 2 tbsp olive oil
- 1/4 cup chicken or fish broth
- 1/4 cup capers
- 1/4 cup lemon juice
- Fresh parsley
- Lemon zest
- Salt and pepper to taste

Substitutions

Substitute halibut

Halibut pan-seared to perfection, dressed in zesty lemon-caper sauce.

Directions

1. Preheat oven.
2. Sear halibut in olive oil.
3. Deglaze with broth; add capers.
4. Squeeze in lemon juice; simmer.
5. Finish with parsley, lemon zest, salt, and pepper.
6. Drizzle sauce over halibut.
7. Unleash the zesty symphony.
8. Elevate your dining experience.

1 person   340   45 mins

Dover Sole Meunière

Ingredients:

- 1 Dover sole fillet
- 1/4 cup all-purpose flour
- 2 tbsp butter
- Lemon juice
- Fresh parsley
- Salt and pepper to taste

Substitutions

Substitute Dover sole

Dover sole, the star of French cuisine, dressed in delicate meunière.

Directions

1. Preheat oven.
2. Dredge sole in flour.
3. Sear sole in butter until golden.
4. Drizzle with lemon juice.
5. Garnish with parsley, salt, and pepper.
6. Revel in the simple elegance.
7. Embrace the French finesse.

1 person | 370 | 50 mins

Grilled Swordfish with Mango Salsa

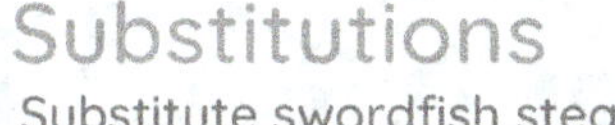

Ingredients:

- 1 swordfish steak
- 2 tbsp olive oil
- 1/4 cup diced mango
- 1/4 cup diced red onion
- 1/4 cup diced bell peppers
- 1/4 cup chopped cilantro
- Lime juice
- Salt and pepper to taste

Substitutions

Substitute swordfish steak

Swordfish takes a tropical twist, crowned with vibrant mango salsa.

Directions

1. Preheat oven.
2. Brush swordfish with olive oil.
3. Grill swordfish until cooked.
4. Mix mango, red onion, bell peppers, cilantro, lime juice, salt, and pepper.
5. Top swordfish with mango salsa.
6. Savor the tropical harmony.
7. Embark on a grilled delight.

Chapter 9:
Healthy and Light

1 person | 280 | 40 mins

Steamed Fish with Ginger and Soy

Ingredients:

- 1 fish fillet (cod, sea bass)
- 2 tbsp soy sauce
- 1 tbsp grated ginger
- 1/4 cup sliced scallions
- Fresh cilantro
- Lime wedges
- Salt and pepper to taste

Substitutions

Substitute fish fillet

A delicate dance of fish with ginger and soy, steamed to perfection.

Directions

1. Preheat oven.
2. Lay fish on steamer.
3. Mix soy sauce and ginger; drizzle over fish.
4. Steam until fish is opaque.
5. Garnish with scallions, cilantro, and lime wedges.
6. Immerse in the delicate dance of flavors.
7. Revel in the simplicity.

1 person | 320 | 45 mins

Baked Lemon-Dill Trout

Ingredients:

- 1 trout fillet
- 2 tbsp olive oil
- Lemon slices
- Fresh dill
- Salt and pepper to taste

Trout baked with zesty lemon and aromatic dill.

Directions

1. Preheat oven.
2. Brush trout with olive oil.
3. Lay lemon slices on trout.
4. Bake until trout is flaky.
5. Garnish with fresh dill.
6. A melody of lemon and dill awaits.
7. Savor the lightness.

Substitutions
Substitute trout fillet

1 person | 310 | 50 mins

Grilled Mediterranean Sea Bream

Ingredients:

- 1 sea bream fillet
- 2 tbsp olive oil
- 1/4 cup diced tomatoes
- 1/4 cup chopped Kalamata olives
- 1/4 cup crumbled feta cheese
- Fresh oregano
- Lemon wedges
- Salt and pepper to taste

Substitutions

Substitute sea bream fillet

A Mediterranean symphony, sea bream grilled to perfection.

Directions

1. Preheat oven.
2. Rub sea bream with olive oil; season.
3. Grill sea bream until cooked.
4. Top with tomatoes, olives, feta, oregano.
5. Serve with lemon wedges.
6. Revel in the Mediterranean harmony.
7. An ode to healthy indulgence.

1 person 290 45 mins

Poached Salmon with Yogurt-Dill Sauce

Ingredients:

- 1 salmon fillet
- 1/4 cup Greek yogurt
- 1 tbsp chopped dill
- Lemon zest
- Lemon juice
- Salt and pepper to taste

Salmon poached to perfection, adorned with tangy yogurt-dill sauce.

Directions

1. Preheat oven.
2. Poach salmon until cooked.
3. Mix yogurt, dill, lemon zest, lemon juice, salt, and pepper.
4. Drizzle yogurt-dill sauce over salmon.
5. Embrace the tangy elegance.
6. A healthy symphony unfolds.

Substitutions
Substitute salmon fillet

1 person | 270 | 40 mins

Herb-Crusted Baked Haddock

Ingredients:

- 1 haddock fillet
- 2 tbsp breadcrumbs
- 1 tbsp chopped parsley
- 1 tbsp chopped thyme
- Lemon zest
- Olive oil
- Salt and pepper to taste

Substitutions

Substitute haddock fillet

Haddock adorned with an aromatic herb crust, baked to perfection.

Directions

1. Preheat oven.
2. Mix breadcrumbs, parsley, thyme, lemon zest, salt, and pepper.
3. Lay haddock on baking sheet.
4. Press breadcrumb mixture onto haddock.
5. Drizzle with olive oil.
6. Bake until haddock is flaky.
7. Revel in the herbaceous charm.
8. A light indulgence awaits.

1 person   340   50 mins

Teriyaki Salmon with Steamed Vegetables

Teriyaki-kissed salmon served with a side of steamed veggies.

Ingredients:

- 1 salmon fillet
- 1/4 cup teriyaki sauce
- 1/4 cup sliced bell peppers
- 1/4 cup sliced zucchini
- 1/4 cup broccoli florets
- 1/4 cup sliced carrots
- Fresh ginger
- Sesame seeds
- Rice
- Salt and pepper to taste

Directions

1. Preheat oven.
2. Marinate salmon in teriyaki sauce.
3. Sear salmon until cooked.
4. Steam bell peppers, zucchini, broccoli, carrots.
5. Top salmon with sesame seeds and ginger.
6. Serve with steamed veggies and rice.
7. A teriyaki journey of lightness.
8. Embrace the balanced flavors.

Substitutions

Substitute teriyaki sauce

1 person | 280 | 40 mins

Lemon-Basil Grilled Tilapia

Ingredients:

- 1 tilapia fillet
- 2 tbsp olive oil
- Lemon zest
- Fresh basil
- Salt and pepper to taste

Tilapia grilled to perfection, kissed by zesty lemon and aromatic basil.

Directions

1. Preheat oven.
2. Rub tilapia with olive oil; season.
3. Grill tilapia until cooked.
4. Top with lemon zest and basil.
5. A melody of lemon and basil unfolds.
6. Savor the lightness.
7. A zesty journey awaits.

Substitutions

Substitute tilapia fillet

1 person

320

50 mins

Citrus-Marinated Grilled Grouper

Grouper marinated in vibrant citrus, grilled to perfection.

Ingredients:

- 1 grouper fillet
- 1/4 cup orange juice
- 1/4 cup lime juice
- 1/4 cup lemon juice
- 1/4 cup chopped cilantro
- Olive oil
- Salt and pepper to taste

Directions

1. Preheat oven.
2. Mix orange juice, lime juice, lemon juice, cilantro, olive oil, salt, and pepper.
3. Marinate grouper.
4. Grill grouper until cooked.
5. A symphony of citrus unfolds.
6. Embrace the vibrant flavors.
7. A taste of healthy indulgence.

Substitutions
Substitute grouper fillet

1 person | 310 | 60 mins

Mediterranean Quinoa Salad with Grilled Fish

Ingredients:

- 1 fish fillet (tilapia, salmon)
- 1/4 cup cooked quinoa
- 1/4 cup diced cucumber
- 1/4 cup diced tomatoes
- 1/4 cup chopped Kalamata olives
- 1/4 cup crumbled feta cheese
- Fresh parsley
- Lemon juice
- Olive oil
- Salt and pepper to taste

Substitutions

Substitute fish fillet

A wholesome feast, grilled fish atop a Mediterranean quinoa salad.

Directions

1. Preheat oven.
2. Grill fish until cooked.
3. Mix quinoa, cucumber, tomatoes, olives, feta, parsley.
4. Drizzle with lemon juice and olive oil.
5. Serve grilled fish atop quinoa salad.
6. A Mediterranean celebration of health.
7. Savor the balanced harmony.

1 person | 260 | 40 mins

Herb-Marinated Grilled Sardines

Ingredients:

- 2 sardine fillets
- 2 tbsp olive oil
- 1/4 cup chopped mixed herbs (parsley, rosemary, thyme)
- Lemon zest
- Salt and pepper to taste

Substitutions
Substitute sardine fillets

Sardines marinated in aromatic herbs, grilled to perfection.

Directions

1. Preheat oven.
2. Mix olive oil, chopped herbs, lemon zest, salt, and pepper.
3. Marinate sardines.
4. Grill sardines until cooked.
5. A herb-infused symphony awaits.
6. Savor the simplicity.
7. A healthy delight for the senses.

Chapter 10:
Global Treasures

1 person | 360 | 60 mins

Icelandic Plokkfiskur (Fish and Potato Hash)

Ingredients:

- 1 fish fillet (cod, haddock)
- 1/4 cup diced potatoes
- 1/4 cup diced onions
- 1/4 cup milk
- Butter
- Nutmeg
- Fresh parsley
- Salt and pepper to taste

A hearty fish and potato hash from the heart of Iceland.

Directions

1. Preheat oven.
2. Sauté potatoes and onions in butter.
3. Add milk, nutmeg, salt, and pepper.
4. Fold in cooked fish and parsley.
5. Let flavors meld.
6. A taste of Iceland's comfort.
7. Savor the rustic delight.

1 person | 290 | 50 mins

Maldivian Garudhiya (Spicy Fish Soup)

Ingredients:

- 1 fish fillet (tuna, grouper)
- 1/4 cup diced onions
- 1/4 cup chopped tomatoes
- 1/4 cup coconut milk
- Curry leaves
- Maldivian chili paste
- Fresh ginger
- Salt to taste

A spicy fish soup that captures the essence of the Maldives.

Directions

1. Preheat oven.
2. Bring onions, tomatoes, coconut milk, curry leaves, chili paste, ginger to a simmer.
3. Add fish; cook until tender.
4. Dive into the Maldivian flavors.
5. Savor the spice.

Substitutions

Substitute fish fillet

1 person | 320 | 60 mins

Argentinian Fish Empanadas

Ingredients:

- 1 fish fillet (hake, sea bass)
- 1/4 cup diced bell peppers
- 1/4 cup diced onions
- 1/4 cup chopped hard-boiled eggs
- Green olives
- Cumin
- Paprika
- Salt and pepper to taste

Argentinian empanadas, filled with the treasures of the sea.

Directions

1. Preheat oven.
2. Sauté bell peppers and onions.
3. Mix cooked fish, eggs, olives, cumin, paprika, salt, and pepper.
4. Assemble empanadas.
5. Bake until golden.
6. Revel in the Argentinian treasure.
7. Savor the flaky delight.

Substitutions
Substitute fish fillet

1 person | 310 | 50 mins

Italian Baccalà alla Livornese

Ingredients:

- 1 salted cod fillet
- 1/4 cup diced tomatoes
- 1/4 cup chopped black olives
- 1/4 cup capers
- Fresh parsley
- Red pepper flakes
- Olive oil
- Salt and pepper to taste

Substitutions
Substitute salted cod fillet

Baccalà alla Livornese, a taste of Italy's coastal heritage.

Directions

1. Preheat oven.
2. Soak cod to remove salt.
3. Sauté tomatoes, olives, capers, red pepper flakes.
4. Add cod; simmer.
5. Drizzle with olive oil; garnish with parsley.
6. A journey to Italy's coast.
7. Savor the Mediterranean zest.

1 person   350   60 mins

Japanese Fish Katsu (Fried Fish Cutlet)

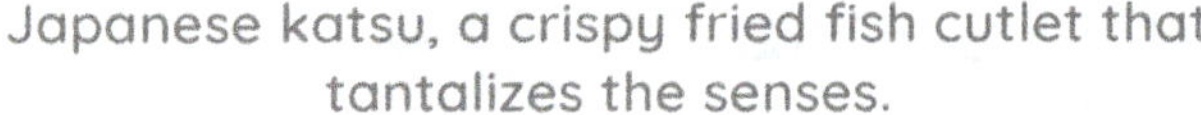

Ingredients:

- 1 fish fillet (white fish)
- 1/4 cup breadcrumbs
- 1/4 cup flour
- 1/4 cup beaten egg
- Tonkatsu sauce
- Cabbage slaw
- Salt and pepper to taste

Japanese katsu, a crispy fried fish cutlet that tantalizes the senses.

Directions

1. Preheat oven.
2. Coat fish in flour, egg, breadcrumbs.
3. Fry until golden.
4. Slice and drizzle with tonkatsu sauce.
5. Serve with cabbage slaw.
6. Embark on a Japanese delight.
7. Savor the crunch.

Substitutions

Substitute fish fillet

1 person | 330 | 60 mins

Tunisian Fish Tagine

Ingredients:

- 1 fish fillet (red snapper, sea bass)
- 1/4 cup diced onions
- 1/4 cup diced tomatoes
- 1/4 cup diced bell peppers
- 1/4 cup diced potatoes
- Harissa paste
- Ground cumin
- Ground coriander
- Fresh cilantro
- Olive oil
- Salt and pepper to taste

Substitutions
Substitute fish fillet

Tunisian tagine, where fish mingles with North African spices.

Directions
1. Preheat oven.
2. Sauté onions, tomatoes, bell peppers, potatoes.
3. Add harissa, cumin, coriander, salt, and pepper.
4. Lay fish on top; drizzle with olive oil.
5. Cover and cook until fish is tender.
6. A tagine journey to Tunisia.
7. Savor the North African spice.

1 person | 280 | 40 mins

Dutch Haringbroodje (Herring Sandwich)

Ingredients:

- 2 herring fillets
- 1/4 cup diced onions
- 1/4 cup chopped pickles
- 1/4 cup mayonnaise
- Fresh dill
- Rye bread
- Salt and pepper to taste

A Dutch delicacy, herring sandwiched between soft bread.

Directions

1. Preheat oven.
2. Clean and fillet herring; chop into small pieces.
3. Mix herring, onions, pickles, mayonnaise, dill, salt, and pepper.
4. Assemble herring mixture on rye bread.
5. A taste of Dutch tradition.
6. Savor the maritime delight.

Substitutions

Substitute herring fillets

1 person | 360 | 60 mins

Brazilian Acarajé with Vatapá (Fish Fritters)

Ingredients:

- 1 fish fillet (white fish)
- 1/4 cup black-eyed pea flour
- 1/4 cup diced onions
- 1/4 cup palm oil
- Ground ginger
- Ground coriander
- Ground red pepper
- Fresh cilantro
- Dried shrimp
- Salt and pepper to taste

Brazilian acarajé, fish fritters filled with the warmth of Brazil.

Directions

1. Preheat oven.
2. Blend fish, flour, onions, ginger, coriander, red pepper, salt, and pepper.
3. Form into fritters.
4. Fry in palm oil until golden.
5. Serve with vatapá sauce.
6. A Brazilian embrace of flavor.
7. Savor the tropical warmth.

Substitutions

Substitute fish fillet

1 person   310   50 mins

Korean Grilled Mackerel (Godeungeo Gui)

Korean grilled mackerel, where fish meets the bold flavors of Korea.

Ingredients:

- 1 mackerel fillet
- 1/4 cup soy sauce
- 1/4 cup chopped scallions
- 1/4 cup minced garlic
- Sesame oil
- Sesame seeds
- Korean red pepper flakes
- Salt and pepper to taste

Directions

1. Preheat oven.
2. Marinate mackerel in soy sauce, scallions, garlic, sesame oil, salt, and pepper.
3. Grill mackerel until cooked.
4. Sprinkle with sesame seeds and red pepper flakes.
5. A Korean symphony of flavors.
6. Savor the spice.

Substitutions

Substitute mackerel fillet

1 person   290   40 mins

Greek Fried Whitebait (Marides Tiganites)

Ingredients:

- Whitebait
- 1/4 cup all-purpose flour
- 1/4 cup chopped fresh herbs (parsley, mint)
- Lemon wedges
- Salt and pepper to taste

Substitutions

Substitute whitebait

Greek marides tiganites, crispy fried whitebait for a taste of Greece.

Directions

1. Preheat oven.
2. Coat whitebait in flour.
3. Fry until crispy.
4. Toss with fresh herbs, salt, and pepper.
5. Serve with lemon wedges.
6. A Greek ode to the sea.
7. Savor the Mediterranean delight.

Chapter 11:
Coastal Inspirations

1 person

340

60 mins

Coastal Fish Stew with Coconut Milk

A coastal delight, fish stew with the creamy embrace of coconut milk.

Ingredients:

- Assorted fish fillets (cod, shrimp, mussels)
- 1/4 cup diced onions
- 1/4 cup diced bell peppers
- 1/4 cup diced tomatoes
- 1/4 cup coconut milk
- Fish stock
- Fresh cilantro
- Lime wedges
- Salt and pepper to taste

Directions

1. Preheat oven.
2. Sauté onions, bell peppers, tomatoes.
3. Add coconut milk, fish stock, salt, and pepper.
4. Simmer until flavors meld.
5. Add fish; cook until tender.
6. Garnish with cilantro and lime wedges.
7. A taste of coastal comfort.
8. Savor the creamy symphony.

Substitutions
Substitute fish fillets

1 person | 380 | 60 mins

Seaside Grilled Seafood Platter

A bountiful grilled seafood platter, a feast from the sea.

Ingredients:

- Assorted seafood (shrimp, squid, scallops)
- 1/4 cup olive oil
- Lemon zest
- Fresh herbs
- Lemon wedges
- Salt and pepper to taste

Directions

1. Preheat oven.
2. Marinate seafood in olive oil, lemon zest, herbs, salt, and pepper.
3. Grill seafood until cooked.
4. Drizzle with olive oil; garnish with lemon wedges.
5. A seaside feast awaits.
6. Savor the bounty.

Substitutions

Substitute seafood

1 person | 350 | 60 mins

Creole Seafood Jambalaya

Ingredients:

- Assorted seafood (shrimp, crawfish, sausage)
- 1/4 cup diced onions
- 1/4 cup diced bell peppers
- 1/4 cup diced celery
- 1/4 cup diced tomatoes
- Cajun seasoning
- Rice
- Fresh parsley
- Salt and pepper to taste

Creole jambalaya, a tantalizing blend of seafood and spices.

Directions

1. Preheat oven.
2. Sauté onions, bell peppers, celery.
3. Add tomatoes, Cajun seasoning, salt, and pepper.
4. Stir in rice.
5. Add seafood; cook until rice is tender.
6. Garnish with parsley.
7. A Creole dance of flavors.
8. Savor the spice.

1 person   320   40 mins

Hawaiian Lomi Lomi Salmon Salad

Ingredients:

- 1 salmon fillet
- 1/4 cup diced tomatoes
- 1/4 cup diced onions
- Fresh scallions
- Fresh herbs
- Salt and pepper to taste

Hawaiian lomi lomi salmon salad, a refreshing taste of the islands.

Directions

1. Preheat oven.
2. Grill salmon until cooked.
3. Dice salmon; mix with tomatoes, onions, scallions, herbs, salt, and pepper.
4. Let flavors meld.
5. A taste of Hawaiian paradise.
6. Savor the freshness.

Substitutions

Substitute salmon fillet

1 person   360   60 mins

Italian Seafood Risotto

Ingredients:

- Assorted seafood (shrimp, calamari, mussels)
- 1/4 cup Arborio rice
- 1/4 cup diced onions
- 1/4 cup white wine
- Fish stock
- Parmesan cheese
- Fresh parsley
- Lemon zest
- Salt and pepper to taste

Substitutions

Substitute seafood

Italian seafood risotto, a luxurious blend of creamy rice and seafood.

Directions

1. Preheat oven.
2. Sauté onions; add Arborio rice.
3. Deglaze with white wine; add seafood.
4. Gradually add fish stock; stir until rice is creamy.
5. Stir in Parmesan, parsley, lemon zest.
6. A journey to Italy's coast.
7. Savor the indulgence.

1 person   330   50 mins

Cajun Blackened Catfish

Ingredients:

- 1 catfish fillet
- Cajun seasoning
- Butter
- Fresh lemon
- Fresh herbs
- Salt and pepper to taste

Cajun blackened catfish, a fiery embrace of flavors.

Directions

1. Preheat oven.
2. Coat catfish in Cajun seasoning.
3. Sear catfish in butter until blackened.
4. Drizzle with lemon juice; garnish with herbs.
5. A Cajun dance of heat and flavor.
6. Savor the spice.

Substitutions
Substitute catfish fillet

1 person   **380**   **60 mins**

Mediterranean Seafood Pasta

Ingredients:

- Assorted seafood (shrimp, mussels, clams)
- 1/4 cup diced tomatoes
- 1/4 cup chopped Kalamata olives
- Fresh basil
- Olive oil
- Red pepper flakes
- Salt and pepper to taste

Substitutions
Substitute seafood

Mediterranean seafood pasta, where pasta meets the treasures of the sea.

Directions

1. Preheat oven.
2. Sauté tomatoes, olives, basil, red pepper flakes.
3. Add seafood; cook until shells open.
4. Toss with cooked pasta.
5. Drizzle with olive oil; season.
6. A Mediterranean embrace of flavors.
7. Savor the symphony.

1 person   340   60 mins

Portuguese Bacalhau à Brás (Cod with Eggs and Potatoes)

Ingredients:

- 1 salted cod fillet
- 1/4 cup diced onions
- 1/4 cup thinly sliced potatoes
- 1/4 cup beaten eggs
- Fresh parsley
- Salt and pepper to taste

Portuguese bacalhau à brás, a blend of cod, eggs, and potatoes.

Directions

1. Preheat oven.
2. Soak cod to remove salt.
3. Sauté onions until golden.
4. Fry potatoes until crispy.
5. Shred cod; stir-fry with onions, potatoes.
6. Add beaten eggs; cook until scrambled.
7. Garnish with parsley.
8. A Portuguese treasure on a plate.
9. Savor the comfort.

Substitutions

Substitute salted cod fillet

1 person | 320 | 50 mins

Thai Seafood Glass Noodle Salad

Ingredients:

- Assorted seafood (shrimp, squid, scallops)
- 1/4 cup glass noodles
- 1/4 cup diced cucumber
- 1/4 cup diced tomatoes
- Fresh herbs
- Lime juice
- Fish sauce
- Thai chili
- Peanuts
- Salt and pepper to taste

Substitutions

Substitute seafood

Thai glass noodle salad, where seafood meets vibrant Thai flavors.

Directions

1. Preheat oven.
2. Marinate seafood; grill until cooked.
3. Soak glass noodles; toss with cucumber, tomatoes, herbs.
4. Dress with lime juice, fish sauce, Thai chili.
5. Top with peanuts.
6. A Thai explosion of taste.
7. Savor the harmony.

1 person | 340 | 60 mins

Moroccan Chermoula Fish Skewers

Ingredients:

- 1 fish fillet (white fish, salmon)
- 1/4 cup chermoula sauce
- Fresh cilantro
- Lemon wedges
- Salt and pepper to taste

Moroccan chermoula fish skewers, a burst of North African flavors.

Directions

1. Preheat oven.
2. Marinate fish in chermoula sauce.
3. Thread fish onto skewers; grill until cooked.
4. Garnish with cilantro; serve with lemon wedges.
5. A Moroccan adventure of flavor.
6. Savor the spice.

Substitutions

Substitute fish fillet

We need your support

As we wrap up this flavor-packed journey, I've got a quick ask, my friends.

If you could spare a moment, consider leaving a review. Those little nuggets of feedback mean the world to us – especially because we're a small crew trying to make a big impact.

Just head back to where you got this book, find that review button, and drop a rating and a sentence. It's like a sprinkle of magic for us. And if you spot a small hiccup along the way – a typo, a tiny slip – know that we've tried our best, and we hope you can look past those little blips.

We're grateful for every review, and we read each and every one. Imagine a bunch of us, huddled around screens, soaking in your thoughts and appreciating the connections we've made through our shared love for food.

As we say farewell for now, here's to many more tasty adventures in your kitchen. Thanks for joining us on this culinary ride, and until next time, happy cooking!